MW01025980

Julie Brooke

Contents

Introduction

The crepe is perhaps the most delicate, the most beautiful and happily for us, one of the easiest meals that can be made. The crepe might summon romantic thoughts of walking through Paris in the sunshine while delighting in a chocolate-covered crepe, yet crepes are simple enough to be made in your own kitchen with ease. They require no fancy equipment and can be cooked fast enough to be ready for any meal in the busiest household. In short, a golden crepe straight from the cooking can be food heaven for everyone and on the table within a few minutes.

The crepe has many talents. Not only does it go wonderfully with chocolate or apples and cinnamon, bananas or blueberries, but it can also be served with cheese or bacon, sausage or egg. The crepe can be created for any meal at any time of the day. Serve a savory crepe for your main course, followed by a sweet crepe for desert. The crepe is not only full of grace, romantic and beautiful but also both practical and versatile.

This recipe book contains 50 of the best recipes you will need to make the perfect crepe for any occasion. Read on now to discover more about how to create the best crepes, the top tips you will need every time and the 50 greatest crepe recipes you will find all in one collection.

Equipment

One of the great aspects of making crepes is their sheer simplicity. You don't need piles of expensive equipment that sits unused in your kitchen most of the time. You can buy crepe makers of course however you don't need one to make crepes at home (although they can be fun to use!). You can make beautiful crepes that taste amazing with just a few basic pieces. If you enjoy baking, it's very likely you have all the tools and equipment already sitting in your kitchen however it is worth going over a few details first just to double check.

Blender or Hand Mix?

It's important to get the batter you are going to use as smooth as possible to avoid creating a lumpy crepe. How you achieve this depends on personal preference and the devices you currently have in your kitchen. Some people find the constant whisking, either by hand or with an electric mixer, to be a chore in which case you might well have a blender already in your home. Simply add all the ingredients into the blender and using brief power pulses, blend until everything is smooth. Use a spatula to ensure all the batter is taken from the sides and fully mixed in.

If you prefer the more traditional way, then continue to use a large mixing bowl or two along with a high-quality whisk. Practice does truly make perfect here and after a while you will find you can create a very smooth batter with a couple of minutes of vigorous whisking. The recipes in this book assume that not everyone has a blender. The final choice is entirely yours however. The end goal is a smooth batter. It doesn't matter if you are using a blender or a whisk with bowls to get there.

Non-stick skillet or pan

At some point, you may wish to consider buying a dedicated crepe pan if you don't already have one. They are not necessary; however, they can make life a little easier in general. They have very low sides which have a gradual slope to them. This makes it easier to get the crepe out onto the plate intact.

Some people prefer the heavier type of pan made of cast iron or stainless steel, others the lighter aluminum pan. I've used both, but I always opt for a non-stick surface however to ensure I have the greatest chance of avoiding wasted crepes and to make the whole process a little easier. Otherwise your pan is a matter of personal preference.

In terms of size, I normally use an 8-inch pan. You can certainly go larger if you like. Lots of people use a 9-inch or even bigger. If you are comfortable with using your normal skillet or pan, then just keep using that. There's no need for any other type of pan when making crepes, although they can be a useful addition to any kitchen and a great gift for a crepe-making fan.

Spatula

You will need a device to extract waffles on occasion from the iron should they stick or be left in too long and burn. A flexible spatula is ideal. Avoid any kind of metal contact that may scratch the non-stick surface of the skillet or pan.

Freezer Containers

It's perfectly fine to make an extra batch of crepes and then freeze them to eat later. Do make sure you separate them with parchment or wax paper before placing them into airtight freezer containers in the freezer, otherwise they will stick together. You can reheat crepes either in the microwave for a quick snack or cover them and heat in the oven for about 10 minutes otherwise.

Ingredients

Crepes are very simple to make and require very few ingredients. Their simplicity and ease of making are one of their main attractions and it's most likely that you currently have all the necessary ingredients in your cupboard right now. The recipes below don't require a lot of rare or expensive ingredients and you can probably get to making your crepes straightaway without needing to head out to the shops.

Here are general points about the ingredients used in the rest of the book.

Butter – assume when the recipes talk about butter, that it is unsalted.

Milk – This comes down to personal choice, but I like to opt for whole milk as I find it a better choice for crepes. Of course, you can go for a lower-fat milk instead if you prefer.

Eggs –In all cases where mentioned, eggs should be assumed to be large.

Flour – I have used unbleached, all-purpose flour for all these recipes. Feel free to experiment a little of course with other variations if you prefer.

Sugar – This is one aspect of the recipes in this book that you can change as you see fit depending on how sweet you like your crepes. The amount of sugar can be altered to suit personal taste both in terms of color and quantity. Where mentioned however, it is assumed to be white sugar unless otherwise specified.

Top 10 Crepe Making Tips

Crepes are easy to make and these tips will ensure you always get the best results. Here are my top 10 tips for the perfect crepe every time!

1.) Resting the batter. Where possible I let the batter sit for 30 minutes or longer in the fridge. This will make your crepes a little lighter and more flavorsome by allowing the gluten in flour to bind effectively with the eggs and milk. However, don't let this stop you making crepes if you are short on time. If I'm running around in a rush making breakfast, I tend to skip this step.

2.) A smooth batter is important for the perfect crepe. One way to help the process is to ensure you sift the flour before adding it. A simple step that will save you lots of time for every batch.

3.) Make more batter! I always tend to make more batter than I need as you will find crepes are so easy to eat they disappear almost as soon as they hit the table. It's easy to double the ingredients and make more on the day. Extra crepes can always be added to the fridge to eat later or frozen for another day.

4.) Heat your pan well first. Ensure the pan is well heated before starting to cook. There's not very much that can go wrong with making crepes, but the crepe will not cook properly and stick to the pan if the pan is not heated all the way through. This is especially important for pans with a heavy bottom. Heat the pan for four to five minutes before using.

5.) Even if using a non-stick surface, I always add a little butter first to the pan. You don't need a huge amount, but it will help in preventing any sticking. You won't need to add butter for every single crepe, but it is important to add enough to cover the base entirely for the first one. Add more butter every five crepes or more if needed.

6.) Consistency. Getting the right consistency of your batter is fundamental to a good crepe. Fortunately, it is easy to change it if not quite right. You are aiming for a consistency just like heavy cream. If you find it a little runny then add more flour by the tablespoon and re-assess once you have whisked it again. If it's too thick, then add more milk, again by the tablespoon, until you reach the desired consistency.

7.) Measurements. The more you make your crepes, the better you will know just how much batter to put into each one for the right level of thickness. Be consistent in your use of a ladle or measuring cup for each crepe so you will always know how much batter to put in. Use something that allows you to add all the batter for a single crepe in one go rather than tablespoon by tablespoon to avoid some of the batter being more cooked than other parts. A measuring cup should do the job perfectly well.

8.) Figuring out exactly when to flip your crepe is more art that science and the time will depend on your pan and heat used. In general however, your crepe will take between a minute and two minutes to cook on one side. It will be ready when the edges of the crepe begin to curl up and the cooked side has gone golden brown.

Flip it over and cook for another 30 seconds to a minute before serving. You're aiming for a light gold color. This will signal the crepe is ready to eat before it becomes a little tough or rubbery to eat. If that is the case, then drop the cooking time down by 20 seconds until you reach the perfect consistency.

9.) The presentation of your crepes can be just as important as any of the above points. If we see a meal that looks beautiful and appealing, we are automatically drawn to it and want to try the dish. Try stacking your crepes or folding them or rolling them around the filling and serving. There are many ways you can present your crepes. Play around and discover what method works best for you and your family.

10.) Experiment. The crepe is an incredibly versatile dish that can cope with a huge range of fillings and ingredients – both sweet and savory. It's the ideal dish to express your own creativity. Experiment for yourself, be adventurous and see what wonderful and magical crepes you can come up with that will quickly become a favorite!

I know you are going to enjoy both creating and then eating all the crepe recipes in this book. Without any further delay, let's start cooking!

Free Gift

I would love to send you an entirely free gift – my Top 100 Cupcake Recipes. This is a whole book dedicated to the wonderful world of cupcakes and contains 100 fantastic, easy to make recipes. If you would like to get a free copy, then just follow the link below and I'll get it out to you straightaway!

Just visit here - http://eepurl.com/bWd-XL - for a free copy of the Top 100 Cupcake Recipes!

CUPCAKE COOKBOOK

TOP 100 CUPCAKE RECIPES

JULIE BROOKE

Apple and Raisin Cinnamon Crepes

There is something wonderfully warming and comforting about apple and cinnamon. Try these crepes for a perfect start to the day or a great dessert in the evening.

Ingredients

1 ½ cups all-purpose flour

3 eggs

1 ½ cups milk

½ teaspoon salt

½ tablespoon butter

2 teaspoons cinnamon

½ teaspoon nutmeg

1 teaspoon vanilla

3 tablespoons sugar

1 tablespoon confectioners' sugar

Filling

2 cups apples, cored and sliced

½ cup raisins

2 tablespoons sugar

Directions

Add the apples, sugar and raisins into a saucepan over medium heat and cook until the apples have softened. Take off the heat while you make the crepes. Add the eggs, vanilla and milk to a bowl and whisk together. Add the flour, salt, cinnamon, nutmeg and sugar to a bowl and mix together. Add the flour bowl to the milk bowl and whisk again until any lumps have disappeared.

Add a little butter to a pan over medium heat followed by enough batter to cover the base. Cook the crepe until golden brown and remove to the plate. Add a tablespoon of the filling down the middle of the crepe and fold over. Serve hot with a sprinkling of confectioners' sugar over the top. Vanilla ice-cream makes a great accompaniment.

Bacon and Parmesan Crepes

I love the more delicate taste of Parmesan cheese with my crepes, especially when combined with the saltiness of bacon. A perfect start to the day – filling and quick and easy to make.

Ingredients

1 ½ cups all-purpose flour

1 cup milk

3 eggs

3 tablespoons Parmesan cheese, grated

1 tablespoon butter, melted

½ teaspoon salt

Filling

½ cup bacon, cooked and chopped

Directions

Start by cooking up the bacon and ensuring it is then cut into small pieces before adding to a bowl Grate the Parmesan and put it to one side. Add the eggs, milk and butter together and whisk. Add the flour, salt and Parmesan into a separate bowl and mix. Add the flour bowl to the egg bowl and mix well until a smooth texture is reached.

Add just a little butter to the pan over a medium heat and then enough batter to cover the base entirely. Cook for a couple of minutes or until golden brown. Remove to the plate, add the bacon to the middle and fold the crepe over itself to serve hot.

Banana Crepes

Bananas go beautifully with most types of breakfast so it come as no surprise that they are perfect in crepes as well.

Ingredients

1 ½ cups all-purpose flour

3 eggs

3 cups milk

2 teaspoons sugar

2 tablespoons melted butter

½ teaspoon salt

4 bananas cut, ripe

1 teaspoon cinnamon

Directions

Melt the butter and leave it to cool slightly. If using a blender, add all the ingredients together and blend well. If mixing by hand, sift in the flour, sugar, cinnamon and salt into a large bowl. Whisk the eggs and together in a separate bowl, gradually add in the flour mixture and mix together. Lastly, add in the melted butter. Cover the bowl and place the batter in the fridge for 30 minutes before starting to cook.

Heat up the frying pan on a medium high heat. Add in around ¼ cup of the mixture into the heated pan and rotate and tilt the pan so the batter coats the entire surface evenly. Cook for two minutes or until the bottom is golden brown. Turn the crepe over and cook the other side. Remove to the plate and add the sliced banana. Fold into halves or even quarters and serve as is or add some cream or ice-cream. You can also sprinkle with some granola for a little extra crunch and top with a very light dusting of cinnamon as well.

Beer Crepes

Beer in a crepe? Why not?! Try these for a change. Beer and milk might not seem the most obvious combination at first, but it certainly works to give a light and airy crepe.

Ingredients

1 ½ cups all-purpose flour

3 eggs

3 cups milk

2 teaspoons sugar

2 tablespoons melted butter

1 teaspoon vanilla

½ teaspoon salt

1 teaspoon vanilla

1 cup semi-sweet chocolate chips

Directions

Start by melting the butter. Combine the butter, milk, eggs and beer into a bowl and mix together. Start to add in the sifted flour and salt slowly while mixing. Ensure the batter is smooth. Cover the bowl and set aside for 30 minutes.

Pour in the batter to a heated pan and cook for two minutes or until golden brown. Turn over and cook the other side until it reaches the same color. Remove from the heat and serve hot.

Blueberry Crepes

Ingredients

1 ½ cups all-purpose flour

3 eggs

3 cups milk

2 teaspoons sugar

2 tablespoons melted butter

1 teaspoon vanilla

½ teaspoon salt

1 cup blueberries

1 tablespoon sugar

¼ cup confectioners' sugar

Directions

Melt the butter and leave it to cool slightly. If using a blender, add all the ingredients together and blend well. If mixing by hand, sift in the flour, sugar and salt into a large bowl. Whisk the eggs and milk together in a separate bowl, gradually add in the flour mixture and mix together. Lastly, add in the melted butter. Cover the bowl and place the batter in the fridge for 30 minutes before starting to cook. Add ½ cup of blueberries and sugar into a pan and just simmer for 15 minutes until the desired syrup consistency is reached. Set aside while you cook the pancakes.

Heat up the frying pan on a medium high heat. Add in around ¼ cup of the mixture into the heated pan and rotate and tilt the pan so the batter coats the entire surface evenly. Cook for two minutes and 30 seconds on the other side. Add to the plate and add the syrup. Top with the remaining blueberries and dust with confectioners' sugar. Serve with cream.

Buttermilk Crepes

Ingredients

1 ½ cups all-purpose flour

3 eggs

2 tablespoons sugar

1 ½ cups buttermilk

1 teaspoon vanilla

½ teaspoon salt

1 tablespoon butter

Topping

Maple Syrup or yogurt

Crushed walnuts or your own favorite nut

Directions

Add the flour, sugar and salt into a bowl and mix well. Add the buttermilk, eggs and vanilla into a bowl and whisk together. Slowly add the flour mix in as well and continue to mix until a smooth batter is reached.

Add just enough batter to a heated pan and cook for no more than two minutes or until a golden brown color is reached. Turn over and cook for a further minute. Cook the batch up while keeping the cooked crepes warm in the oven or just covered.

Add two or three crepes to the plate, fold them over each other to form a triangle and serve with yogurt or maple syrup and a crushed nut of your choosing.

Cannoli Crepes

Ingredients

1 ½ cups all-purpose flour

2 cups milk

3 eggs

¼ teaspoon salt

½ teaspoon vanilla

1 tablespoon butter

1 tablespoon sugar

Filling

2 cups ricotta cheese

1 teaspoon vanilla

½ cup semi-sweet chocolate chips

½ cup confectioners' sugar

½ teaspoon cinnamon

Directions

Make the cream by adding all the filling ingredients into a bowl or food processor and mixing well. Set the filling to one side while you make the crepes. Add the milk, eggs, vanilla and butter together and whisk. In a separate bowl, add the flour and salt and add into the egg bowl. Mix until the batter is smooth. Add a little more butter to the pan and add enough mixture to coat the pan entirely. Cook for a couple of minutes. Turn the crepe over and cook for another minute before transferring to a plate. Add a large tablespoon of the filling down the middle and fold the crepe over. Cover with some further powdered sugar and top with a couple of chocolate chips. Delicious!

Caramel Apple Crepes

Hot caramel sauce simply works with crepes with the flavors of crepe and sauce complementing each other perfectly.

Ingredients

1 ½ cups all-purpose flour

3 eggs

3 cups milk

2 teaspoons sugar

2 tablespoons melted butter

½ teaspoon salt

Sauce

1 cup brown sugar

½ cup butter

2 cups apples, sliced and cored

2 teaspoons vanilla

½ teaspoon nutmeg

Directions

Start with the sauce by melting the ½ cup butter and then adding the brown sugar and apples into a saucepan. Cook over a medium high heat in a covered pan until the apples gradually begin to soften and become tender. This will a little less than 10 minutes. Uncover the saucepan now and carry on cooking for another 10 minutes. Add in the vanilla and nutmeg and stir carefully before setting aside.

Melt the butter and leave it to cool slightly. If using a blender, add all the ingredients together and blend well. If mixing by hand, sift in the flour, sugar and salt into a large bowl. Whisk the eggs and milk together in a separate bowl, gradually add in the flour mixture and mix together. Lastly, add in the melted butter. Cover the bowl and place the batter in the fridge for 30 minutes before starting to cook.

Heat up the frying pan on a medium high heat. Add in around $\frac{1}{4}$ cup of the mixture into the heated pan and rotate and tilt the pan so the batter coats the entire surface evenly. Cook for two minutes or until the bottom is golden brown. Turn the crepe over and cook the other side before removing to a plate. Add the sauce to cover the crepe and serve as is or topped with a nut of your choice and cream. If you have any of the sauce left over, then freeze to use next time.

Carrot Cake Cream Cheese Crepes

Ingredients

1 ½ cups all-purpose flour

2 cups milk

3 eggs

2 ½ cups carrots, peeled and chopped

1 tablespoon sugar

¼ teaspoon salt

1 teaspoon cinnamon

½ teaspoon nutmeg

Filling

1 package cream cheese, 8 ounces

1 cup confectioners' sugar

1 tablespoon milk

Directions

Add the chopped carrots into a blender along with half a cup of milk. Blend the carrots continuing to add the rest of the milk until the lumps have disappeared. Finally, add the eggs and blend again. Empty the contents of the blender into a bowl. Add the flour, sugar, salt, cinnamon and nutmeg into a new bowl and mix together. Gradually add the flour bowl into the wet ingredients and mix well. Cover and add to the fridge for an hour.

Make the filling by combining the cream cheese with the sugar. Add a little more sugar to thicken or a little more milk to make it runnier until you have the right consistency.

Add a little butter to a pan over medium heat and add enough batter to cover the base. Cook for a couple of minutes and then a further 30 seconds on the other side. Remove to a plate and add about a tablespoon of the filling. Fold over the crepe and then sprinkle a little more confectioners' sugar over the top of the crepe to serve. Add chopped fruit if your own choosing as an optional accompaniment.

Cheese and Ham Crepes

These are delicious and so flavorsome. Make them for dinner and follow up with the sweet crepes for a guaranteed hit.

Ingredients

1 ½ cups all-purpose flour

3 eggs

3 cups milk

1 cup grated cheddar cheese

Sliced ham

2 tablespoons melted butter

½ teaspoon salt

Directions

Preheat the oven to 325F. Melt the butter and leave it to cool slightly. If using a blender, add all the ingredients together and blend well. If mixing by hand, sift in the flour, sugar and salt into a large bowl. Whisk the eggs and milk together in a separate bowl, gradually add in the flour mixture and mix together. Lastly, add in the melted butter. Cover the bowl and place the batter in the fridge for 30 minutes before starting to cook.

Heat up the frying pan on a medium high heat. Add in around ¼ cup of the mixture into the heated pan and rotate and tilt the pan so the batter coats the entire surface evenly. Cook for two minutes or until the bottom is golden brown. Turn the crepe over and cook the other side before removing to a plate to cool.

Add on two slices of ham to each crepe following by cheese and then roll up. Place each rolled up crepe into a greased baking dish and add any remaining cheese over the top. Bake for about 15 minutes or until the cheese has melted and serve hot.

Cheesecake and Berry Crepes

I love just about every variety of cheesecake so creating a recipe that combines both cheesecake and crepes was a joy. Try this recipe for a wonderful fusion of both cheesecake and crepe.

Ingredients

1 ½ cups all-purpose flour

2 ½ cups milk

4 eggs

2 tablespoons sugar

¼ teaspoon salt

1 tablespoon butter

Confectioners' sugar for topping

Filling

1 package cream cheese, 8 ounces

2 tablespoons confectioners' sugar

1 teaspoon vanilla

3 cups of sliced berries (raspberry or strawberry taste amazing)

Directions

Add the cream cheese and vanilla to a bowl with the confectioners' sugar. Add more sugar if necessary to thicken or a little water or milk to lighten if necessary. Fold in the berries and set aside. Add the milk and eggs to a bowl and whisk together. Add the flour, sugar and salt to another bowl and mix together. Add the flour bowl to the milk bowl and mix until a smooth batter is reached.

Add some butter to the pan and place on a medium heat. Add enough batter to cover the base and cook for a couple of minutes or until golden brown. Turn over and cook for another 30 seconds to a minute. Add about 1 ½ tablespoons of the filling to each crepe and fold over itself. Top with a little more filling or a conserve and finally some confectioners' sugar.

Chicken and Avocado Crepes

This is a great savory meal for lunch or later in the day. Create these and then move on to the sweet crepe for dessert!

Ingredients

1 ½ cups all-purpose flour

3 eggs

1 ½ cups milk

½ teaspoon salt

1 tablespoon butter

Filling

2 chicken breasts, cooked and diced

1 avocado

½ cup Parmesan, grated

1 cup sugar

1 lime, cut

Directions

Cook the chicken first and dice. Prepare the avocado by removing the stone, adding the avocado flesh to a bowl and mashing it lightly. It doesn't need to be completely smooth. Add the diced chicken to the avocado and stir in.

Add the eggs and milk to bowl and whisk together. In a separate bowl, add the flour and salt and then add this to the milk bowl. Mix well until a smooth batter is gained. Add a little butter to a pan over medium heat and enough batter to cover the base. Cook for a couple of minutes or until golden brown before turning over for a further 30 seconds. Cook all the batter and keep the previously cooked crepes in a warmed over.

Add two crepes to a plate and add a full tablespoon of the chicken and avocado mix. Add the Parmesan over the filling. Fold the crepes over. Extract the juice from the lime and pour over for a great brunch-time treat.

Chocolate Chips Crepes

This is a firm favorite in our household and I suspect we are not unique. Chocolate and crepes have gone together for a very long time and for good reason. Try these now to see for yourself.

Ingredients

1 ½ cups all-purpose flour

3 eggs

3 cups milk

1 teaspoon sugar

2 tablespoons melted butter

1 teaspoon vanilla

½ teaspoon salt

1 teaspoon vanilla

1 ½ cups semi-sweet chocolate chips

Directions

In a new saucepan, melt the butter and leave it to cool slightly. If using a blender, add all the ingredients together and blend well. If mixing by hand, sift in the flour, sugar and salt into a large bowl. Whisk the eggs, vanilla and milk together in a separate bowl, gradually add in the flour mixture and mix together. Lastly, add in the melted butter. Cover the bowl and place the batter in the fridge for 30 minutes before starting to cook.

Melt ½ cup chocolate chips either in a microwave or in a glass bowl over a pan of boiling water and set to one side while you cook the crepes. Heat up the frying pan on a medium high heat. Add in around ¼ cup of the mixture into the heated pan and rotate and tilt the pan so the batter coats the entire surface evenly. Cook for two minutes or until the bottom is golden brown. Turn the crepe over and cook the other side for about a minute.

While still hot, transfer the crepe to the plate. Spread the cream down the middle and sprinkle on the chocolate chips. Fold over the crepe tightly so the chips begin to melt into the cream. Drizzle the melted chocolate over the crepe and serve. You can add a little sprinkle of confectioners' sugar as well or serve with some extra fruit on the side.

Chocolate Hazelnut Crepes

If you happen to be wandering the streets of Paris, you will find these being offered on practically every corner. They are however simple to make in your own kitchen and just as delicious. You may not be able to see the Eiffel Tower every day, but you can still have the crepe!

Ingredients

1 ½ cups all-purpose flour

3 eggs

3 cups milk

2 tablespoons melted butter

½ teaspoon salt

1 cup chocolate hazelnut spread

Topping

Banana, sliced

1 cup cream, whipped

Directions

Melt the butter and leave it to cool slightly. If using a blender, add all the ingredients together and blend well. If mixing by hand, sift in the flour and salt into a large bowl. I find these more than sweet enough so normally remove the sugar when making. Whisk the eggs and milk together in a separate bowl, gradually add in the flour mixture and mix together. Lastly, add in the melted butter. Cover the bowl and place the batter in the fridge for 30 minutes before starting to cook.

Heat up the frying pan on a medium high heat. Add in around ¼ cup of the mixture into the heated pan and rotate and tilt the pan so the batter coats the entire surface evenly. Cook for two minutes or until the bottom is golden brown. Remove from the heat to a plate and add chocolate hazelnut spread throughout the middle of the crepe.

At this point, you can add the sliced banana as well to the middle if you love the chocolate and banana combination (I do!). Roll up the crepe and return to the heat just for a minute with the lesser cooked side facing outwards.

Serve with cream and additional banana slices if preferred along with whipped cream.

Cinnamon and Buckwheat Crepes

Ingredients

1 ½ cups buckwheat flour

½ teaspoon salt

3 eggs

1 cup milk

2 tablespoons sugar

2 teaspoons cinnamon

½ tablespoon butter

Topping

Yogurt

Directions

Add the flour, salt and cinnamon into a bowl and mix. In a new bowl, add the eggs and milk and whisk together. Add in the flour bowl and continue to mix until you gain a smooth batter.

Place a pan over medium heat and add enough batter to cover the base of the pan entirely. Cook for a couple of minutes or until golden brown. Turn over and cook for a further 30 seconds to a minute. Add to the plate and serve as it is or with yogurt drizzled over the top.

Classic Crepes

This recipe produces about 12 beautifully thin and crisp crepes that will be devoured. The sheer simplicity makes them a delight and they can be eaten for breakfast, lunch or dinner. These are for desert crepes so you may wish to remove the sugar if adding a savory topping. From preparation to the cooking, it's no more than 30 minutes.

Ingredients

1 ½ cups all-purpose flour

3 eggs

3 cups milk

2 teaspoons sugar

2 tablespoons melted butter

½ teaspoon salt

Directions

Melt the butter and leave it to cool slightly. If using a blender, add all the ingredients together and blend well. If mixing by hand, sift in the flour, sugar and salt into a large bowl. Whisk the eggs and milk together in a separate bowl, gradually add in the flour mixture and mix together. Lastly, add in the melted butter. Cover the bowl and place the batter in the fridge for 30 minutes before starting to cook.

Heat up the frying pan on a medium high heat. Add in around ¼ cup of the mixture into the heated pan and rotate and tilt the pan so the batter coats the entire surface evenly. Cook for two minutes or until the bottom is golden brown. Turn the crepe over and cook the other side before serving hot.

Cocoa Crepes

These are lovely and simple. I find these sweet enough already with the addition of the cocoa, but you can always add a little more sugar as well if you prefer.

Ingredients

1 ½ cups all-purpose flour

3 eggs

3 cups milk

1 cup cocoa powder

1 teaspoon vanilla

1 cup cream, whipped

Directions

Melt the butter and set to one side. If using a blender, add all the ingredients together and blend well. If mixing by hand, sift in the flour into a large bowl. Whisk the eggs, vanilla and milk together in a separate bowl, gradually add in the flour mixture and mix together. Add in the melted butter. Cover the bowl and place the batter in the fridge for an hour.

Heat up the frying pan and add a little of the batter ensuring it covers all the pan. Cook for about 90 seconds to 2 minutes and then flip over to cook for another minute at most. Remove to a plate, add the cream to the middle and fold over. You can add a little confectioners' sugar or even extra cocoa powder sprinkled over the top as well for a final touch of decadence.

Cream Cheese Crepes

These are light and easy to make. You can have them plain or add a little fruit or drizzle with honey for a glorious and cheery breakfast. Mix it up and experiment to find the perfect combination. I tend to make lots of the filling and add to the fridge to reuse the next day if any is left.

Ingredients

1 ½ cups all-purpose flour

3 eggs

3 cups milk

2 teaspoons sugar

2 tablespoons melted butter

1 teaspoon vanilla

½ teaspoon salt

1 teaspoon vanilla

Honey or fruit to taste

Filling

16 ounces cream cheese

1 cup powdered sugar

1 teaspoon vanilla

2 tablespoons milk

2 teaspoons vanilla

Directions

Start with the filling by adding the cream cheese, powdered sugar and vanilla into a bowl and mixing until all smooth. You can do this by hand or an electric mixer if easier. If it gets a little thick then use the milk. If it gets too runny, then add more powdered sugar. Set aside while you make the crepes.

In a new saucepan, melt the butter and leave it to cool slightly. If using a blender, add all the ingredients together and blend well. If mixing by hand, sift in the flour, sugar and salt into a large bowl. Whisk the eggs, vanilla and milk together in a separate bowl, gradually add in the flour mixture and mix together. Lastly, add in the melted butter. Cover the bowl and place the batter in the fridge for 30 minutes before starting to cook.

Heat up the frying pan on a medium high heat. Add in around ¼ cup of the mixture into the heated pan and rotate and tilt the pan so the batter coats the entire surface evenly. Cook for two minutes or until the bottom is golden brown. Turn the crepe over and cook the other side for about a minute.

While still hot, transfer the crepe to the plate. Spread the filling down the middle of the crepe and fold over. Serve hot either as they are or with a topping of fruit or honey. They are just as good with a dusting of confectioners' sugar and a cup of coffee.

Crepe Suzettes

A recipe that's been around a long time and one that I hope will continue to be so for a long time yet. A real winner for every type of guest at a dinner party. Feel free to change up the alcoholic part of the recipe to your personal favorite.

Ingredients

1 ½ cups all-purpose flour

3 eggs

3 cups milk

2 teaspoons sugar

2 tablespoons melted butter

1 teaspoon vanilla

½ teaspoon salt

Sauce

½ cup butter

4 tablespoons sugar

Juice from 3 large oranges, freshly squeezed

Zest – 1 orange

1 ½ tablespoons Cointreau

Directions

Start with the sauce by adding the orange juice to a saucepan followed by the butter, sugar, orange zest and Cointreau. Once it has started to boil over a low heat then let it simmer gently. The sauce will start to thicken after about 15 minutes.

Melt the butter and leave it to cool slightly. If using a blender, add all the ingredients together and blend well. If mixing by hand, sift in the flour, sugar and salt into a large bowl. Whisk the eggs and milk together in a separate bowl, gradually add in the flour mixture and mix together. Lastly, add in the melted butter. Cover the bowl and place the batter in the fridge for 30 minutes before starting to cook.

Heat up the frying pan on a medium high heat. Add in around ¼ cup of the mixture into the heated pan and rotate and tilt the pan so the batter coats the entire surface evenly. Cook for two minutes or until the bottom is golden brown. Turn the crepe over and cook the other side before removing to the serving dish.

Once they have all been cooked, pour the syrup all over the heap of pancakes. Swirl each pancake around to ensure it has a liberal coating of the sauce and serve to a delighted group of friends.

Eggnog Crepes

I always ensure I make more eggnog than I ever need at Christmas time just so I can make these crepes with them. A real treat without which Christmas isn't quite Christmas anymore!

Ingredients

2 cups eggnog

3 eggs

3 tablespoons butter, melted

1 ½ cups all-purpose flour

1 teaspoon salt

1 tablespoon nutmeg

3 tablespoons sugar

Confectioners' sugar

Directions

Add the eggnog, eggs and butter into a bowl and mix. In a separate bowl, add the flour, salt, nutmeg and sugar and mix well. Gradually add to the eggnog mixture and mix together until you have a smooth batter.

Add a little butter to a pan and heat. Add enough batter to cover the entire pan and cook for a couple of minutes or until golden brown. Turn over and cook for another 30 seconds before removing to a plate, adding sugar and serve hot.

Ginger Crepes

Ginger is another flavour commonly associated with Christmas, but just like the Eggnog recipe above, these are great at any time of the year.

Ingredients

1 ½ cups all-purpose flour

2 eggs

1 ½ cups milk

1 teaspoon cinnamon

2 teaspoons ginger, ground

½ teaspoon salt

2 tablespoons sugar

Topping

1 cup heavy cream, whipped

Maple Syrup

Confectioners' sugar

Directions

Add the eggs and milk to a bowl and whisk together. Add the flour, salt, cinnamon, ginger and salt to a bowl and mix. Add the flour bowl to the milk bowl and whisk until any lumps have disappeared.

Add enough batter to a heated pan to cover the base and cook until golden brown. Cook the entire batch in one go, keeping the cooked crepes warm in the over. Serve 2 or 3 at a time on a plate and cover with the cream, topped up by maple syrup and a little confectioners' sugar.

Glazed Pear Crepes

Ingredients

1 ½ cups all-purpose flour

2 cups milk

3 eggs

2 tablespoons butter, melted

2 tablespoons sugar

¼ teaspoon salt

Filling

2 pears, sliced

4 tablespoons butter

1 teaspoon brown sugar

1 teaspoon cinnamon

Directions

Prepare the filling first by adding the sugar, butter pears and cinnamon into a saucepan and cooking until the sugar is dissolved and the pears have softened completely. This will take about 7 to 8 minutes. Set aside to cool slightly while you make the crepes. Add the milk, eggs and butter together and mix well. In another bowl, add the sifted flour, salt and sugar and mix. Add the flour bowl to the milk bowl slowly and mix until a smooth batter is reached.

Add a little butter to the pan over a medium heat and enough batter to cover the base of the pan. Rotate and twist the pan to ensure it is all covered. Cook for two minutes or until golden brown. Place two or three crepes together on the plate and carefully add the cooked pears with their juices over the top. You can serve with a little vanilla ice-cream or yogurt for an extra treat.

Granola and Berry Crepes

Ingredients

1 ½ cups all-purpose flour

3 eggs

3 cups milk

2 tablespoons melted butter

½ teaspoon salt

1 tablespoon sugar

Filling

1 cup granola

½ cup yogurt

1 tablespoon honey or maple syrup

1 cup fresh fruit (bananas or any berry works well)

Confectioners' sugar

Directions

Add the eggs and milk and 1 tablespoon of butter into a bowl and whisk together. In a separate bowl, add the flour, salt and sugar and mix. Add the flour bowl to the eggs gradually and mix well until a smooth batter is reached.

Use the remaining butter to cook the crepes. Add a little each time to a pan over medium heat followed by enough batter to cover the base. Cook for a couple of minutes or until golden brown and then another 30 seconds on the side.

Add two crepes to a plate and then add the yogurt, followed by the granola, the fresh fruit and finally the honey or maple syrup. Sprinkle with just a little confectioners' sugar to serve.

Herb and Eggs Crepes

Egg and crepes is a great savory crepe. Mix up your choice of herbs or go for a combination to produce a subtly different crepe each time.

Ingredients

1 ½ cups all-purpose flour

3 eggs

3 cups milk

2 tablespoons melted butter

½ teaspoon salt

½ cup fresh herbs (choose chives or basil or parsley as examples)

½ cup grated Parmesan cheese

Filling

4 eggs

1 tablespoon milk

Salt and pepper

1 tablespoon butter

Directions

Add the eggs, milk and melted butter into a bowl and mix together. In a separate bowl and the flour and salt and add to the egg bowl.

Finally, add the cheese and herbs of your choice. Mix well, cover and leave for an hour.

Start cooking by adding some more butter to a pan, followed by enough batter to cover the base. Cook for a couple of minutes until a golden color is reached and then turn over for a further 30 seconds. Cook the entire amount and place in a pre-heated oven to remain warm.

To make the filling, add all the ingredients to a bowl and whisk together. Add to a pan and let it sit for 30 seconds. Stir gradually from the outside into the middle of the pan. Remove from the heat while still a little runny. They will continue to cook off the heat and inside the crepe.

Add the filling down the middle of a crepe, fold the crepe over itself and serve.

Honey and Ricotta Crepes

Ingredients

1 ½ cups all-purpose flour

2 cups milk

3 eggs

2 tablespoons butter, melted

1 tablespoon sugar

¼ teaspoon salt

Filling

1 cup ricotta

4 tablespoons honey

Optional fruit of your choice

Directions

Add the milk, eggs and butter together and mix well. In another bowl, add the sifted flour, salt and sugar and mix. Add the flour bowl to the milk bowl slowly and mix until a smooth batter is reached. In a separate bowl, add the ricotta and honey and whisk together.

Add a little butter to the pan over a medium heat and enough batter to cover the base of the pan. Rotate and twist the pan to ensure it is all covered. Cook for two minutes or until golden brown. Turn over the crepe and cook for another minute at the most.

Remove to the plate and add a dollop of the ricotta and honey mix. Fold the pancake over and drizzle a little more honey over the top. You can eat as is or combine with your favorite chopped fruit.

Honeyed Butter and Walnuts Crepes

Ingredients

1 ½ cups all-purpose flour

3 eggs

3 cups milk

2 teaspoons sugar

2 tablespoons melted butter

1 teaspoon vanilla

½ teaspoon salt

8 tablespoons butter (make sure this is at least room temperature)

½ cup honey

1/3 cup walnuts, crushed

Directions

Start off by melting the butter and leave it to cool slightly. If using a blender, add all the ingredients together and blend well. If mixing by hand, sift in the flour, sugar and salt into a large bowl. Whisk the eggs and milk together in a separate bowl, gradually add in the flour mixture and mix together. Lastly, add in the melted butter. Cover the bowl and place the batter in the fridge for 30 minutes before starting to cook.

Heat up the frying pan on a medium high heat. Add in around ¼ cup of the mixture into the heated pan and rotate and tilt the pan so the batter coats the entire surface evenly. Cook for two minutes or until the bottom is golden brown. Turn the crepe over and cook the other side for about a minute.

While still hot, transfer the crepe to the plate. Add a generous helping of butter all the way down the middle of the crepe followed by the honey. Fold the crepe over tightly so the heat will melt away the already soft butter into the crepe. Pour a little extra honey over the top along with some crushed walnuts (or your favorite nut) and serve hot.

Lemon Crepes

One of the simplest, yet most adored recipes in cuisine, the lemon crepe is a true work of art. These are best served piping hot with liberal helpings of lemon and sugar.

Ingredients

1 ½ cups all-purpose flour

3 eggs

3 cups milk

2 teaspoons sugar

2 tablespoons melted butter

½ teaspoon salt

Topping

Sugar with lemon wedges

Directions

Melt the butter and leave it to cool slightly. If using a blender, add all the ingredients together and blend well. If mixing by hand, sift in the flour, sugar and salt into a large bowl. Whisk the eggs and milk together in a separate bowl, gradually add in the flour mixture and mix together. Lastly, add in the melted butter. Cover the bowl and place the batter in the fridge for 30 minutes before starting to cook.

Heat up the frying pan on a medium high heat. Add in around ¼ cup of the mixture into the heated pan and rotate and tilt the pan so the batter coats the entire surface evenly. Cook for two minutes or until the bottom is golden brown. Turn the crepe over and cook the other side before adding to the plate, two at a time. Drench in lemon juice, sprinkle with sugar and serve with the lemon wedge on the side!

Mango Crepes

This recipe produces about 12 beautifully thin and crisp crepes that will be devoured. The sheer simplicity makes them a delight and they can be eaten for breakfast, lunch or dinner. From preparation to the cooking, it's no more than 30 minutes.

Ingredients

1 ½ cups all-purpose flour

3 eggs

3 cups milk

2 teaspoons sugar

2 tablespoons melted butter

½ teaspoon salt

2 cups mangoes, diced and drained

1 teaspoon ginger

1 teaspoon cinnamon

1 cup cream, whipped

Directions

Add the mango, ginger and cinnamon into a bowl and mix well together before setting side. Melt the butter and leave it to cool slightly. If using a blender, add all the ingredients together and blend well. If mixing by hand, sift in the flour, sugar and salt into a large bowl. Whisk the eggs and milk together in a separate bowl, gradually add in the flour mixture and mix together. Lastly, add in the melted butter. Cover the bowl and place the batter in the fridge for 30 minutes before starting to cook.

Heat up the frying pan on a medium high heat. Add in around ¼ cup of the mixture into the heated pan and rotate and tilt the pan so the batter coats the entire surface evenly. Cook for two minutes or until the bottom is golden brown. Turn the crepe over and cook the other side. Add the crepe to a plate, add whipped cream down the middle and top with the mango made previously. Serve with additional mango and cream covering the crepe.

These go particularly well I find with a cup of coffee or white wine if you are feeling particularly decadent.

Matcha Crepes

I adore the color of these as well as the taste. If you want something a little different, then these are just perfect

Ingredients

1 ½ cups all-purpose flour

2 eggs

2 tablespoons Matcha

1 cup milk

1 cup cream, whipped

Confectioners' sugar

½ cup of butter

Directions

Add the Matcha, salt and flour into a bowl and combine. In a separate bowl, add the 2 eggs and milk. Slowly add in the flour bowl and whisk vigorously as you go to produce a smooth texture. Melt a little butter in a pan and then add in the batter, enough just to cover the base of the pan entirely. Cook for a minute, then turn over and cook for no more than 30 seconds or so. Remove each crepe to a plate ensuring they stay warm as you do.

To serve, place one or two crepes on a plate and fold in half. Add some cream to the top and sprinkle with confectioners' sugar for a beautiful desert.

Mocha Crepes

Ingredients

1 ½ cups all-purpose flour

1 tablespoon cocoa powder, unsweetened

1 teaspoon espresso powder

2 eggs

1 cup milk

1 tablespoon sugar

½ teaspoon salt

1 teaspoon vanilla

½ cup of butter

Confectioners' sugar

Sauce

3 tablespoons brewed coffee

½ cup cocoa powder

1 teaspoon vanilla

1 cup sugar

Directions

Start with the mocha sauce by adding the ingredients to a saucepan and heating until you reach the boil. Remove from the heat to cool slightly while you prepare the crepes.

Add the cocoa, sugar, espresso powder, salt and flour into a large bowl and mix together. In a separate bowl, add the eggs, milk, butter and eggs and whisk together. Add in the flour bowl into the eggs and continue to whisk well until you have a smooth batter. If using a blender, then combine all the ingredients and blend together.

Add a little more butter to a pan to heat up and then add just enough batter to cover the surface of the pan. Cook for about 2 minutes, turn and cook the other side for another minute. Remove to a serving dish to create a stack of crepes and once you cooked all of them, smother the pile with the mocha sauce. Serve hot with a covering of confectioners' sugar.

Oat and Almond Crepes

These taste delicious, feel healthy and will fill you up as well. Perfect for a breakfast for any busy family.

Ingredients

1 cup oats

1 cup almond meal

1 cup all-purpose flour

2 cups milk

2 eggs

1 teaspoon vanilla

1 ½ tablespoons sugar

½ teaspoon salt

Optional Topping

Chopped fruit

Yoghurt

Directions

Add the almond meal and oats into a food processor and grind them together until you get the same consistency as flour. Add this into a large bowl and add in the flour, followed by the salt and sugar. In a new bowl, add the eggs, milk and vanilla and whisk. Add in the flour bowl to the egg bowl and mix again until you have a smooth batter.

Place a pan over medium heat and add enough batter to cover the base of the pan entirely. Cook for a couple of minutes or until golden brown. Turn over and cook for a further 30 seconds to a minute. Remove to the plate and serve simply as it is or perhaps with some chopped fruit and yogurt of your choice.

PB and J Crepes

Anything with peanut butter is an automatic winner in my household. These are no exception and there won't be any left to freeze afterwards!

Ingredients

1 ½ cups all-purpose flour

3 eggs

3 cups milk

2 teaspoons sugar

2 tablespoons melted butter

1 teaspoon vanilla

½ teaspoon salt

½ cup peanut butter

½ cup favorite jam

1 cup of favorite fruit, chopped

Directions

Melt the butter and leave it to cool slightly. If using a blender, add all the ingredients together and blend well. If mixing by hand, sift in the flour, sugar and salt into a large bowl. Whisk the eggs and milk together in a separate bowl, gradually add in the flour mixture and mix together. Lastly, add in the melted butter. Cover the bowl and place the batter in the fridge for 30 minutes before starting to cook.

Heat up the frying pan on a medium high heat. Add in around ¼ cup of the mixture into the heated pan and rotate and tilt the pan so the batter coats the entire surface evenly. Cook for two minutes or until the bottom is golden brown. Turn the crepe over and cook the other side before removing to the plate.

Take a generous dollop of peanut butter and spread liberally down the middle of the crepe. Top with whatever flavour of jam you fancy followed by a fruit – I love mine with bananas again. Fold the crepe over the filling and fold in the crepe to create a cylinder like effect. Cut into three sections before serving hot.

Peach Crepes

Ingredients

1 ½ cups all-purpose flour

3 eggs

3 cups milk

2 teaspoons sugar

2 tablespoons melted butter

1 teaspoon vanilla

½ teaspoon salt

1 teaspoon vanilla

¼ teaspoon nutmeg

¼ teaspoon cinnamon

Sauce

Juice from 3 oranges, freshly squeezed

Zest from 1 orange

1 tablespoon Amaretto

4 peaches, sliced

1 cup cream, whipped

Directions

Add the orange juice, orange zest and Amaretto to a saucepan and place over a medium heat until it starts to boil. Remove from the heat and allow to cool slightly while you make the crepes. In a new saucepan, melt the butter and leave it to cool slightly. If using a blender, add all the ingredients together and blend well. If mixing by hand, sift in the flour, sugar, nutmeg, cinnamon and salt into a large bowl. Whisk the eggs, vanilla and milk together in a separate bowl, gradually add in the flour mixture and mix together. Lastly, add in the melted butter. Cover the bowl and place the batter in the fridge for 30 minutes before starting to cook.

Heat up the frying pan on a medium high heat. Add in around ¼ cup of the mixture into the heated pan and rotate and tilt the pan so the batter coats the entire surface evenly. Cook for two minutes or until the bottom is golden brown. Turn the crepe over and cook the other side for about a minute.

While still hot, transfer the crepe to the plate. Add some whipped cream down the middle, followed by the sliced peach and fold over the crepe. Pour the sauce over the top, add some more sliced peaches over the top and serve.

Pineapple Crepes

Ingredients

1 ½ cups all-purpose flour

3 eggs

3 cups milk

2 teaspoons sugar

2 tablespoons melted butter

1 teaspoon vanilla

½ teaspoon salt

1 teaspoon vanilla

¼ teaspoon cinnamon

Confectioners' sugar

Sauce

1 large can pineapple chunks

3 tablespoons butter

½ cup sugar

½ teaspoon cinnamon

Directions

Add the butter, sugar and cinnamon into a pan and bring to the boil.
Reduce the heat and cook for another 10 minutes or until the sauce

thickens. Add in the pineapple chunks, stir and remove from the heat.

In a new saucepan, melt the butter and leave it to cool slightly. If using a blender, add all the ingredients together and blend well. If mixing by hand, sift in the flour, sugar, cinnamon and salt into a large bowl. Whisk the eggs, vanilla and milk together in a separate bowl, gradually add in the flour mixture and mix together. Lastly, add in the melted butter. Cover the bowl and place the batter in the fridge for 30 minutes before starting to cook.

Heat up the frying pan on a medium high heat. Add in around $1/4$ cup of the mixture into the heated pan and rotate and tilt the pan so the batter coats the entire surface evenly. Cook for two minutes or until the bottom is golden brown. Turn the crepe over and cook the other side for about a minute.

While still hot, transfer the crepe to the plate. I prefer to serve this with nothing inside and the sauce with pineapple poured over the top. The glistening pineapple sauce always looks both beautiful and delicious. Serve hot with the lightest dusting of confectioners' sugar over the top.

Plum Crepes

Ingredients

1 ½ cups all-purpose flour

2 cups milk

3 eggs

¼ teaspoon salt

½ teaspoon vanilla

½ teaspoon cinnamon

1 tablespoon butter

1 tablespoon sugar

Filling

1 8-ounce packet cream cheese

½ cup confectioners' sugar

1 pound plums, pitted and sliced

1 tablespoon butter

½ tablespoon sugar

½ teaspoon cinnamon

Directions

Add the butter, plums, sugar and cinnamon into a pan over medium heat and cook for about 10 minutes. The plums will soften up and their juices will thicken. Remove from the heat but keep in the pan to stay warm while you make the crepes. Add the confectioners' sugar to the cream cheese, beat well together and set aside.

Add the milk, butter, eggs and vanilla to a bowl and whisk together. Add the flour, salt, sugar and cinnamon together and mix well. Add the flour mix to the milk bowl and mix again until smooth. Add a little butter to a pan over medium heat and add enough batter to cover the bottom of the pan entirely. Cook for two minutes until golden brown and then turn over for another 30 seconds.

Remove two or three crepes to the plate creating a folded pile. Add the cream cheese to one side and cover the stack of crepes with the warm plums and the thickened juice.

Potato Crepes

If you're wondering what to do with any leftovers, then why not make a crepe from the potatoes!

Ingredients

1 cup mashed potato

3 eggs

1 cup milk

2 tablespoons butter

½ teaspoon salt

Pinch of pepper

½ cup flour

Topping

½ cup grated cheese

Directions

Add the eggs and milk to a bowl and mix together. Add in the flour, butter salt and pepper and mix well. Not add in the mashed potato and whisk. This may take a while, but preserve until you get a smooth batter. Cover and leave to sit for an hour.

Add a little butter to a pan over medium heat followed by enough batter to cover the pan. Cook for a little under two minutes before turning over for a further 30 seconds to a minute on the other side. You can serve with a little grated cheese over the top for a great savory meal.

Pumpkin Crepes

Ingredients

½ cup pumpkin puree

2 teaspoons pumpkin pie spice

3 tablespoons sugar

½ teaspoon cinnamon

4 eggs

1 cup milk

½ teaspoon salt

1 ½ cups all-purpose flour

1 teaspoon vanilla

½ cup butter

Filling

1 package cream cheese, 8 ounces

2 cups icing sugar

Topping

1 cup semisweet chocolate, melted

Directions

Prepare the filling by combining the cream cheese and icing sugar well. If it gets too thick, then add a little milk. Set to one side and melt the chocolate in the microwave or in a glass bowl over boiling water. Set to one side also while you make the crepes.

Add the eggs, milk, vanilla and pumpkin puree to a bowl and whisk together. In a separate bowl, mix the flour, cinnamon, salt and pumpkin pie spice and add gradually to the bowl of wet ingredients. Mix well until a smooth batter is reached. Cover and leave for 30 minutes to an hour.

Heat a pan with a little butter in and pour enough mixture in to cover the base rotating the frying pan to ensure it is all covered. Cook for about a minute before turning over the other side for another minute.

Remove to a plate and add the cream-cheese filling before folding the crepe over itself. Drizzle the melted chocolate over the top and serve.

Rainbow Crepes

These are so much fun to make and perfect for a party. You don't have to go for the colors of a rainbow, sometimes just 3 slices of color can look very effective. Mix it up and experiment yourself for your preferred combination

Ingredients

3 cups all-purpose flour

6 eggs

4 tablespoons sugar

½ cup butter, melted

3 cups milk

2 teaspoons vanilla

Food coloring – various

Confectioners' sugar

Filling

1 package cream cheese, 8 ounces

2 cups icing sugar

Directions

Add the eggs, milk, vanilla and butter into a bowl and mix well. Add in the sifted flour gradually and combine well until all is smooth. If using a blender, then add all the ingredients together and blend together. You may have to do that a couple of times due to the increased quantities.

You now need to separate the batter out to the number of colors you would like. If you go for the full rainbow effect, you will want 7 bowls. Add the desired food coloring to each bowl. Before you start to cook, prepare the filling by adding the cream cheese and icing sugar together. If it gets too thick, you can add a little water.

Cook up the batter for each bowl by adding just enough each time to cover the pan and cooking for about 2 minutes on one side and a minute on the other side. Add the crepes to a plate and use the filling in between layers to ensure the stability of your creation. The full rainbow order would be red, orange, yellow, green, blue, indigo and violet.

Once you have made your stunning stack of crepes then add some confectioners' sugar over the top and serve to your appreciative audience.

Red Velvet Crepes

These look delicious on any plate. Serve with a cream cheese filling and a drizzle of chocolate over the top for the finishing touch.

Ingredients

1 ½ cups all-purpose flour

½ teaspoon baking soda

½ teaspoon baking powder

2 tablespoons cocoa powder, unsweetened

2 cups milk

½ cup buttermilk

3 eggs

1 teaspoon vanilla

2 tablespoons sugar

½ tablespoon red food coloring (or a little more if you want it darker red)

1 tablespoon butter, melted

Filling

1 can cream cheese, 8 ounces

½ cup powdered sugar

Topping

½ cup dark chocolate chips

Directions

Prepare the filling by combining the cream cheese with the confectioners' sugar. Add a little more sugar if not quite thick enough or a little milk if too runny. Prepare the topping by melting the chocolate in the microwave or in a glass bowl over boiling water and set aside.

Add the flour, baking soda, salt, baking powder and cocoa powder into a bowl and mix together. In a separate bowl, add the milk, buttermilk, vanilla, eggs, sugar, coloring and butter. Mix together and then gradually add the flour bowl in mixing until you have a smooth batter. Set aside for 30 minutes.

Heat a little butter in a pan over medium heat. Add enough batter to cover the entire pan and cook for about 2 minutes. Flip the crepe over and cook for another minute before removing to a plate. Add the filling down the middle of the crepe and fold the crepe over itself. Drizzle a little chocolate over the top for a stunning desert that tastes as good as it looks.

Rhubarb and Cream Crepes

Ingredients

1 ½ cups all-purpose flour

3 eggs

2 tablespoons sugar

1 ½ cups milk

1 teaspoon vanilla

½ teaspoon salt

1 tablespoon butter

Topping

1 pound rhubarb (fresh or defrosted from frozen)

1 cup sugar

1 teaspoon vanilla

1 cup heavy cream, whipped

Directions

Start with the topping by preparing your rhubarb. If cooking defrosted it will already be prepared, but otherwise remove the tops and bottom and then cut into thin slices a little under an inch each. Add the rhubarb into a saucepan along with the sugar and vanilla and let it reach the boil. Leave it covered and simmering on a lower heat for 7 to 8 minutes until it has softened. Remove from the heat entirely while you make the crepes.

Add the eggs, milk and vanilla to a bowl and whisk together. Add the flour, sugar and salt to another bowl and mix. Add the flour bowl to the milk bowl and continue to whisk until a smooth batter appears.

Add some butter to a heated pan over medium heat and enough batter so the entire base is covered. Cook for a couple of minutes or until a golden brown color is reached. Turn over and cook for a further 30 seconds to a minute. Cook the entire batch this way, adding the cooked crepes to the over so they stay warm.

Once completed, add two or three crepes to a plate and cover with the cooked rhubarb. These go perfectly with heavy cream or some vanilla ice cream on the side.

S'Mores Crepes

Ingredients

1 ½ cups all-purpose flour

2 cups milk

4 eggs

2 tablespoons butter, melted

2 tablespoons sugar

1 cup graham crackers, crushed

1 cup semi-sweet chocolate chips

1 cup mini marshmallows (or marshmallow spread if you prefer)

¼ teaspoon salt

Directions

Add the eggs, milk and butter together and mix together. Add the sifted flour, salt and sugar together into a bowl. Add the flour bowl to the egg bowl and mix well until the batter is smooth. Add enough mixture to a greased or buttered pan to cover the entire base. Cook for a couple of minutes and turn over for a further 30 seconds.

Remove to the plate and start with a thick layer of cracker crumbs. Add on the marshmallows and chocolate chips and fold up quickly to melt the contents. Add a few more chocolate chips over the top and serve with some ice-cream just as it comes.

Salted Caramel Crepes

The silky look of hot caramel topping is so attractive, you won't have any left for the freezer from this recipe. It's an incredible combination – crepe and caramel were made to go together!

Ingredients

1 ½ cups all-purpose flour

2 cups milk

3 eggs

¼ teaspoon salt

1 tablespoon butter

1 tablespoon sugar

Topping

1 ½ cups sugar

½ cup water

1 cup heavy cream

1 teaspoon salt (large flaked)

½ cup unsalted butter

Directions

Add the sugar from the topping to a pan over medium heat followed by the water and whisk it continuously until it has melted. It will reach a dark brown color at which point add the butter. Be careful here as everything will bubble up rapidly. Carry on whisking until the butter has melted and remove from the heat. Now add the cream. Watch out again for everything rising suddenly. Continue with the whisking until everything is well mixed. Now add the salt and whisk for the final time.

To make the crepes, add the milk, eggs and butter together and mix well. In a separate bowl, add the flour, salt and sugar and mix. Add the flour mix to the milk bowl and mix well until the batter is smooth. Add a little butter to a pan over medium heat and then enough batter to cover the base of the pan. Cook until golden brown before turning over and cooking for another 30 seconds to a minute. Remove from the heat to a plate before covering in the salted caramel sauce to serve.

Sausage and Egg Crepes

Simple, but delicious and nourishing. A great breakfast for the whole family.

Ingredients

1 ½ cups all-purpose flour

2 cups milk

3 eggs

¼ teaspoon salt

1 tablespoon butter

Filling

2 onions

1 pound pork sausage roll

1 cup cheddar cheese, grated

¼ teaspoon salt

Pinch of pepper

1 tablespoon butter

Directions

Prepare the filling by adding the butter, chopped onion, salt, pepper and sausage to a frying pan and cooking until the sausage meat is ready. Add in the cup of cheese and carry on cooking until the cheese has melted in. Set to one side keeping the mixture in the pan.

Add the milk, eggs and butter together and whisk. In a separate bowl, add the flour and salt and add into the egg bowl. Mix until the batter is smooth. Add a little more butter to the pan and add enough mixture to coat the pan entirely. Cook for a couple of minutes. Turn the crepe over and cook for another minute before transferring to a plate.

Add 2 tablespoons of the mixture down the middle of the crepe before folding over itself and serving hot.

Smoked Salmon with Cream Cheese Crepes

These are lovely and delicate and can go equally well cut into smaller pieces and handed out as finger food at parties. The salmon complements the delicate and light-flavored crepe perfectly.

Ingredients

1 ½ cups all-purpose flour

3 cups milk

3 eggs

2 tablespoons butter, melted

½ teaspoon salt

Filling

½ tablespoon lemon juice

3 scallions

½ pound smoked salmon

½ cup cream cheese

Chives or dill

Directions

Start with the filling by adding the lemon juice and chopped scallions to the cream cheese and mixing well. Put this into the fridge for an hour or so. Once done, add the eggs, milk and butter together and whisk. Add the flour and salt and mix well until a smooth texture is reached. Add just a little butter to the pan over a medium heat and then enough batter to cover the base entirely. Cook for a couple of minutes or until golden brown.

Place the cooked crepe onto a plate. Add the cream cheese mixture down the middle of the crepe, followed by the smoked salmon slice. Fold up tightly and garnish with chives or dill as decoration.

Spinach and Feta Crepes

Ingredients

1 ½ cups all-purpose flour

3 eggs

3 cups milk

2 tablespoons melted butter

½ teaspoon salt

Filling

½ cup onion chopped

3 cups spinach, fresh

1 teaspoon lemon juice

Salt and Pepper

1 1/2 cups feta cheese

Directions

Add the eggs, butter and milk to a bowl and whisk together. In a separate bowl, add the flour and salt and then add the flour mix to the egg bowl. Mix well until you have a smooth batter. Add a little butter to a pan over medium heat and enough batter to cover the base. Cook for a couple of minutes until golden brown.

Once done, start with the filling by adding the onions to a pan over medium heat and cooking until they soften. Cut off any stems from the spinach and add it to the pan so any moisture evaporates. Remove add to a bowl along with the lemon juice and 1 cup of feta.

Add about a tablespoon or a little more to each crepe and fold it over itself. Add all the crepes to baking dish and crumble the remaining half cup of feta over the top. Add the dish to the oven at a medium heat and bake for 15 minutes before serving.

Strawberry Cream Crepes

These are a real family favorite and can be made with fresh or frozen strawberries. They have a lovely delicate flavour which is only heightened with the addition of a good vanilla ice-cream I find. They also look beautiful!

Ingredients

1 ½ cups all-purpose flour

3 eggs

3 cups milk

2 teaspoons sugar

2 tablespoons melted butter

1 teaspoon vanilla

½ teaspoon salt

1 tablespoon sugar

Filling

3 cups strawberries, chopped

1 package cream cheese

1 cup confectioners' sugar

1 teaspoon vanilla

1 cup cream, whipped

Directions

Start with the filling by adding the cream cheese and confectioners' sugar into a bowl with vanilla. Add in a little over 2 cups of strawberries, saving the rest for a garnish, and mix together. Fold in the cream and set aside

Melt the butter and leave it to cool slightly. If using a blender, add all the ingredients together and blend well. If mixing by hand, sift in the flour, sugar and salt into a large bowl. Whisk the eggs and milk together in a separate bowl, gradually add in the flour mixture and mix together. Lastly, add in the melted butter. Cover the bowl and place the batter in the fridge for 30 minutes before starting to cook.

Heat up the frying pan on a medium high heat. Add in around ¼ cup of the mixture into the heated pan and rotate and tilt the pan so the batter coats the entire surface evenly. Cook for two minutes or until the bottom is golden brown. Turn the crepe over and cook the other side remove to a cooling rack. Add the filling down the middle and then roll up the crepe. Serve with additional strawberries on top and ice-cream as an optional extra.

Tiramisu Crepes

Ingredients

1 ½ cups all-purpose flour

2 cups milk

3 eggs

¼ teaspoon salt

1 tablespoon butter

1 tablespoon sugar

2 teaspoons espresso powder

1 teaspoon cocoa powder

Filling

½ cup mascarpone

1 tablespoon sugar

1 teaspoon vanilla

Directions

To make the filling, add the mascarpone, vanilla and sugar together and beat well before setting to one side. Add the milk, butter and eggs into a bowl and whisk together. In a separate bowl, add the flour, salt, sugar, espresso and cocoa powders and mix together. Add this bowl to the milk bowl continuing to mix until a smooth batter is reached.

Add a little more butter to a pan over medium heat before adding enough batter to cover the pan. Cook for a couple of minutes or until golden brown and turn over for a further 30 seconds or on the other side. Remove to a plate. Add a tablespoon of the filling and fold up the crepe to serve

Tuna and Sweetcorn Crepes

Ingredients

1 ½ cups all-purpose flour

3 eggs

1 ½ cups milk

½ teaspoon salt

½ tablespoon butter

Filling

½ cup onion, chopped

2 cans tuna, drained

1 can sweetcorn, drained

2 tablespoons mayonnaise

½ cup cheddar cheese, grated

Directions

Add all the chopped onion, tuna, sweetcorn and mayonnaise together and mix well before setting aside. Add the eggs and milk together and whisk. In a separate bowl, add the sifted flour and salt before adding to the milk bowl and whisking again.

Add a little butter to a pan over medium heat followed by enough batter to cover the base. Cook for a couple of minutes or until golden brown before turning over for a further 30 seconds. Remove to the plate and add a heaped tablespoon of filling down the middle of the crepe. Sprinkle some cheese over the top of the filling, fold the crepe over itself and serve.

Vanilla and Raspberry Crepes

Ingredients

1 ½ cups all-purpose flour

2 cups milk

3 eggs

2 tablespoons sugar

3 teaspoons vanilla

¼ teaspoon salt

1 tablespoon butter

Confectioners' sugar (for topping)

Filling

2 ½ cups raspberries

1 cup sugar

2 teaspoons lemon juice

Directions

Keeping half a cup of raspberries back, add 2 cups of raspberries, the sugar and the lemon juice to a pan and bring to a boil over medium heat. Continue to cook until the sugar has completed melted away. Keeping the lid on, simmer for a few minutes until it thickens. Remove from the heat to cool slightly while you make the crepes.

Add the milk, eggs and vanilla to a bowl and whisk together. In a new bowl, add the flour, sugar and salt and mix together. Add the flour bowl to the milk bowl gradually and continue to whisk well until a smooth batter is reached.

Add some butter to a pan over medium heat and enough batter to cover the base of the pan. Cook for a couple of minutes or until golden brown and turn over for a further 30 seconds on the other side. Remove to a plate and add a tablespoon of the filling down the middle of the crepe. Cover the crepe and add some further fresh raspberries and confectioners' sugar over the top for a delicious and beautiful dessert.

Yogurt and Apricot Crepes

Ingredients

1 ½ cups all-purpose flour

2 cups milk

4 eggs

3 tablespoons butter, melted

2 tablespoons sugar

1 teaspoon vanilla

¼ teaspoon salt

1 cup apricots, pitted and sliced

Filling

1 cup Greek yogurt

½ teaspoon vanilla

1 tablespoon sugar

Directions

Make the filling first by combing the yogurt, vanilla and sugar and mixing well together. Set the filling aside while you make the crepes. Add the eggs, vanilla, milk and butter together and mix together. Add the sifted flour, salt and sugar together into a different bowl. Add the flour bowl to the egg bowl and mix well until the batter is smooth. Add the batter to a greased or buttered pan to cover the entire pan. Cook for a couple of minutes and turn over for a further 30 seconds.

Add the cooked crepe to a plate and add the filling you made before. Add some apricots in and then cover over itself. Add a little more the filling over the top and serve.

Made in the USA
Monee, IL
26 November 2022

18606915R00049